DISASTER!
HURRICANES

By Dennis Brindell Fradin

Consultant:
Robert C. Sheets, Ph.D.
Meteorologist

 CHILDRENS PRESS, CHICAGO

This satellite view of Hurricane Anita was taken on September 1, 1977.

For my editor, Joan Downing

For their help, the author thanks:

Don Witten, Public Affairs Officer, National Weather Service
Parnell and Jessie McKay, editors and publishers of the
Pass Christian Tarpon-Beacon

Library of Congress Cataloging in Publication Data

Fradin, Dennis B.
  Hurricanes.

  (Disaster!)
  Summary: Discusses the conditions that
cause hurricanes to form and the precautions
that should be taken against them. Also
describes some famous hurricane disasters,
including Camille, which hit the Gulf States
in August, 1969.
  1. Hurricanes—Juvenile literature.
[1. Hurricanes. 2. Gulf States—Hurricane,
1969] I. Title. II. Series: Fradin, Dennis B.
Disaster!
QC944.F7   551.5'52   81-38553
ISBN 0-516-00852-8   AACR2

TABLE OF CONTENTS

Satellite view of Hurricane Camille taken on Sunday, August 17, 1969.

1/CAMILLE - 1969

The storm wasn't spectacular when it was born on August 5, 1969. On satellite pictures it appeared merely as a cloud patch moving west from Africa. During the next several days, its winds increased and it dropped heavy rains on the Leeward Islands. It wasn't a hurricane yet, however. A storm must have winds of at least 74 miles per hour to earn that name.

As the storm approached the United States, the National Hurricane Center sent up airplanes to study it. On August 15, the storm's winds were measured at over 100 miles per hour. It was named "Hurricane Camille."

On the evening of August 15, Camille slammed into Cuba. It battered that island with high winds and ten inches of rain. When Camille was through with Cuba, three people were dead. The hurricane then headed for the southeastern coast of the United States.

Over the warm waters of the Gulf of Mexico, Camille grew stronger than ever. On August 16, weather experts who flew into Camille clocked its winds at 160 miles per hour. That day the National Hurricane Center called for a *hurricane watch* extending along the coast from St. Marks, Florida to Biloxi, Mississippi. The hurricane watch meant that coastal residents should prepare for the possibility of the storm striking land within two days. Residents gassed up their cars in case they had to leave in a hurry. Then they turned on their radios and television sets to learn exactly where Camille was expected to hit.

Later on August 16 the hurricane watch was changed to a *hurricane warning*. The warning meant that the hurricane was expected to strike a specific place within the next twelve hours. Scientists thought that Camille's target would be northwest Florida.

Camille surprised the experts. The storm's forward movement began to slow down about 350 miles south of Panama City, Florida. Camille barely moved for hours. When it began churning forward again, the hurricane was headed right for the Mississippi coast.

On Sunday, August 17, new hurricane warnings informed Mississippi coastal residents of Camille's approach. Early that afternoon, an airplane flying inside Camille clocked its winds at more than 200 miles per hour. Those tremendous winds— plus huge waves—were expected to smash the Mississippi shore by evening. People who turned on their radios and television sets heard this message:

EXTREMELY DANGEROUS CAMILLE CONTINUES TO MOVE TOWARD THE MOUTH OF THE MISSISSIPPI RIVER… PREPARATIONS AGAINST THIS EXTREMELY DANGEROUS HURRICANE SHOULD BE COMPLETED WITHIN THE NEXT FEW HOURS. WINDS ARE INCREASING AND TIDES ARE RISING… TIDES UP TO 15 FEET ARE EXPECTED…EVACUATION OF THE LOW-LYING AREA THAT WILL BE AFFECTED BY THESE TIDES SHOULD BE DONE AS EARLY AS POSSIBLE BEFORE ESCAPE ROUTES ARE CLOSED…HEAVY RAIN WITH LOCAL AMOUNTS OF 8 TO 10 INCHES WILL SPREAD INTO SOUTHEASTERN MISSISSIPPI…HIGHEST WINDS ARE ESTIMATED AT 160 MILES PER HOUR NEAR THE CENTER…

Throughout the afternoon, thousands of people left their beachfront homes and went inland. Police and Civil Defense officials traveled along the Mississippi coastline advising those remaining to leave. Gerald Peralta, police chief of Pass Christian, Mississippi, went door to door. "A hurricane's coming tonight," he explained. "It's expected to have winds of 175 to 200 miles per hour and it may produce waves of ten feet."

Hurricane Camille damaged many Pass Christian, Mississippi beachfront homes.

Most people listened to Peralta and left their beachfront homes. But some refused to leave.

"This is a three-story building—we can go up to the third floor if a wave comes," residents of the Richelieu Apartments told Peralta.

"Not if the first two floors cave in," Peralta answered.

Peralta made trip after trip to the Richelieu Apartments. He finally convinced all but about two dozen people to leave.

By evening, 100,000 persons along the Gulf Coast had left their homes. Those who remained thought that there might be a little flooding and some broken windows. They had no idea that they were about to be struck by one of the mightiest hurricanes in United States history.

Richard I. Hadden, Sr.

Camille first touched the Mississippi coast at about nine in the evening. "The wind was the worst noise I have ever heard in my life," remembered Richard I. Hadden, an attorney who lived in Pass Christian, Mississippi. "It sounded like a thousand freight trains and a thousand airplanes coming right at you. It was horrendous—enough to deafen you."

The tremendous winds tore off roofs, ripped up buildings, and hurled cars through the air. Trees that had been planted long before the Civil War were torn out as if they were only weeds being pulled from the ground. The limbs were sent hurtling like spears through windows and roofs. The 200-mile-per-hour winds of Camille were among the strongest ever measured in a hurricane. And they blew hour after hour. But the wind wasn't the greatest killer in Camille.

Have you ever seen the wind create small waves on a pond or lake? Camille's mighty winds created tremendous walls of water on the Gulf of Mexico. The water rose as much as twenty-five feet. Ten- to fifteen-foot waves on top crashed into the coastal cities. Buildings were washed right off their foundations. As the buildings were ripped apart, the people inside were thrown into the swirling waters. Some jumped in to avoid being trapped inside sinking houses.

Richard Hadden swam to a boat that was tied up in his back yard. Hadden survived by spending six hours on the upside-down boat. Other people held onto rooftops, mattresses, and floating debris. Some climbed trees.

Flash floods and mud slides in the wake of Hurricane Camille caused widespread damage. This house in Roseland, Virginia was ripped off its foundation.

Pat and Sam Maxwell

The Richelieu Apartments in Pass Christian were ripped to shreds by the huge waves and terrific winds. About twenty people who had ignored Police Chief Peralta's warnings perished. Only three people at the apartments survived—one a five-year-old boy who floated to safety on a mattress.

Throughout the night, people floating on wreckage fought for their lives. Then, before dawn, the wind lessened and the water began its return to the Gulf of Mexico.

The dazed survivors came down from trees, rooftops, and attics. "Our town looked like a set from a disaster movie," said Pat Maxwell of Long Beach, Mississippi. She and her husband had survived the hurricane by spending the night in their attic. "Trees were down, cars were upside down, and houses were wrecked. Two bodies were jammed against our house. A car that smashed against the house had torn a hole in the wall. Our belongings—and all kinds of things—were scattered all over."

"I've lived in Long Beach all my life and I got lost as we walked the mile toward downtown," said her husband, Sam Maxwell. Sam had served as mayor of the town for seven years. "I was lost because trees, buildings, and landmarks were gone. There was no way to tell one street from another."

*The Richelieu Apartments in Pass Christian before and after Hurricane Camille.
Only three people who stayed at the apartments survived the hurricane.*

Mississippi's Gulf Coast looked as if it had been hit by a huge bomb. Bodies, bricks, trees, furniture, and railroad tracks lay strewn about. Many things could be seen where they didn't belong. In Biloxi, a shrimp boat was perched on some railroad tracks. In Gulfport, a boat that had been carried several blocks inland sat in front of the First Baptist Church.

The animal kingdom was greatly disturbed by Camille. Thousands of dead pets and farm animals were found among the human bodies. Deer, muskrats, and other wild animals lay drowned. Untold millions of fish were dead. Living animals wandered about, dazed. At Pascagoula, Mississippi, thousands of water moccasins invaded the town. These poisonous snakes had been driven out of the flooded rivers and marshes. An alligator that had been driven from a Louisiana bayou was seen wandering about in the town of Bay St. Louis, Mississippi. At Waveland, Mississippi, a porpoise floundered helplessly on the beach. A man and several children pushed it back into the water.

The people along the Gulf Coast were in great need of help. Thousands were without homes, clothes, food, money, or drinking water. The Red Cross, the Salvation Army, the United States government, and volunteer groups came in to help. Food, water, and medicine were sent in. People were given clothes to wear and a place to sleep. But it took families months or even years to rebuild their homes.

Once a hurricane reaches land, it weakens. Most experts thought that after Camille battered the Mississippi coast its killing days were over. As Camille churned northeastward, its winds did lessen. But the hurricane's clouds still carried tons of water. On the night of August 19-20, tremendous rainstorms assaulted Virginia and West Virginia. In Nelson County, Virginia, twenty-seven inches of rain fell in eight

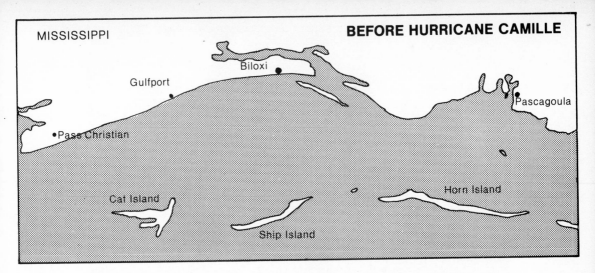

Biloxi

Gulfport

•Pass Christian

Pascagoula

Cat Island

Horn Island

Ship Island

*Maps of Mississippi had to be changed after Hurricane Camille. Ship Island,
twelve miles off the coast, was cut in half by the hurricane-driven waters.
The three-mile gap between the two sections of the island was named "Camille Cut."*

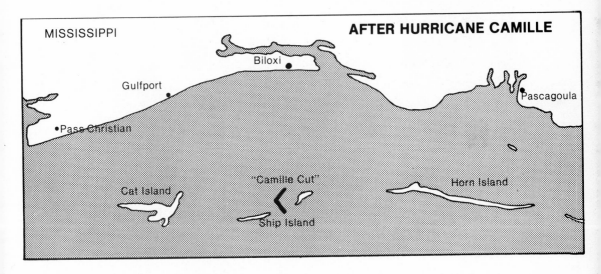

MISSISSIPPI   **AFTER HURRICANE CAMILLE**

Biloxi

Gulfport

•Pass Christian

Pascagoula

Cat Island

"Camille Cut"

Horn Island

Ship Island

hours. In other places, a foot of water fell. The water caused
rivers to flood, washed away bridges and houses, and created
mud slides. Most people were sleeping. They had no warning.
More than 100 died in these floods, raising Camille's United
States death toll to 324.

On August 20, Hurricane Camille returned to the ocean
where it had been born. Its winds dropped to 65 miles per
hour and then less. Off the coast of Newfoundland, Camille
disappeared. But those who had experienced its howling
winds and raging waters would never forget Camille.

The force of Hurricane Camille twisted steel beams (above) and ripped
buildings off their foundations. Before the hurricane, a three-story
apartment building rested on the foundation shown in the picture below.

2/SURVIVORS - CAMILLE, 1969

Many reminders of Hurricane Camille still can be found along the Mississippi Gulf Coast. There are trees bent and twisted out of shape by the storm. There are slab foundations on which houses once stood. And there are people who were lucky enough to survive the storm. Here are the stories of several of those survivors:

Jacqueline and Leon Hines - Gulfport, Mississippi

"All of our neighbors had gone—we were the only ones left in the neighborhood," Jacqueline Hines explained twelve years after Camille. "People called us up and told us to leave. My husband, Leon, wanted to go, but I was the fool. I thought maybe the windows would be knocked out and we'd get a little water. I had experienced other hurricanes without anything very bad happening. I had no idea that this time the whole Gulf of Mexico would come up over our house."

At the time of Camille, Jacqueline Hines was a fifty-nine-year-old gymnastics and dancing teacher. She worked for the Gulfport Recreational Department. Leon, sixty-two years old, worked in a men's clothing store. They lived in a pretty house several hundred feet from the Gulf of Mexico.

"It started raining about six o'clock in the evening and the electricity went off at about that time," Jacqueline Hines remembered. "The wind started whipping around. At first it just broke little bitty twigs, but then as it got stronger, it broke branches. Meanwhile the rain got heavier and heavier."

The couple thought they would be able to leave if things got really bad. Their car was parked in the carport. But at about eight-thirty they heard a loud crash. Leon Hines went to investigate. "We can't get the car out anymore!" he told his wife. A large tree had blown down and now lay blocking their car.

"At about nine-thirty I was in the front room looking out the window when water started coming under the door and into the house," Jacqueline Hines continued. "I yelled: 'Leon, we'd better get out of here!' I tried other doors but couldn't get any open. Then I realized that we were trapped in there. The water continued to come into the house. And within five minutes it was waist deep.

"Water rose up as high as the windows and broke them out—and suddenly a gush of water came and washed glass, bricks, and us right out of the house."

Leon and Jacqueline Hines described their Hurricane Camille experience during a television interview with Charles Bronson and Jill Ireland.

Mr. and Mrs. Hines half-swam and half-scrambled to the 60-foot-tall television antenna that stood in a block of cement outside their house. "The water was neck deep by the time we got to the antenna," Jacqueline Hines continued. "We started climbing up the antenna but the water was still rising. We had to climb higher and higher as the water rose. I saw water go over the top of our house and then I couldn't even see the roof of our house. It was under water."

Jacqueline and Leon Hines were halfway up the antenna — about 30 feet off the ground — and they were still in water. "Lightning flashed across the sky and I could see limbs from trees flying by," said Jacqueline Hines. "I saw our television sail through the air and I saw our refrigerator bobbing away on the water.

"The crash of the thunder and the roar of the wind were horrible. The wind was blowing so hard that I couldn't breathe, and I had trouble just holding my head up. At some points, I felt I couldn't hold on any longer."

After clinging to the television antenna for about two hours, Jacqueline and Leon Hines felt it start to bend. The terrified couple realized that it was cracking at the bottom. When it broke off, they were dropped deep under the chilly water.

Jacqueline Hines was an expert swimmer. She fought her way up above the surface. As the lightning flashed, she looked for her husband. "Leon! Leon! Leon!" she cried. But he was nowhere to be seen. "I knew he had to be under water, so I went under again and kicked something soft. Leon was about eight feet below the surface. I caught him by the collar, hooked him with my foot, and pulled him up."

Swimming in the deep water, Jacqueline Hines struggled to keep herself and her husband afloat. Although Leon Hines

The hurricane completely demolished the home of Jacqueline and Leon Hines.

was only unconscious, his wife didn't yet know whether he was alive or dead.

"The current was so strong that it was just like being out in mid-ocean," said Jacqueline Hines. "I swam and held him up for I don't know how long. Then I saw that our roof had come off the house and was floating like a barge. Leon came to and started helping himself and we were able to make it to the roof.

"We hung onto the roof until about three-thirty in the morning, when the water went down. Then we slid off the roof and onto the ground."

Except for the foundation slab, the Hines's house was gone. They crawled over bricks and other debris to a neighbor's house. At dawn, the Civil Defense came to look for survivors. "Anybody here?" they shouted.

"We're here!" Jacqueline Hines answered.

The couple was taken for medical treatment. Leon had a crushed right shoulder, a concussion, a blood clot on his hip, and a multitude of cuts and bruises. Jacqueline had two broken ribs, several broken bones in her foot, and cuts on her face.

They lived in a small apartment for a year and a half before moving into another house. Today they live in that house, which stands several blocks from the water. "I'll never be that stupid again," said Jacqueline Hines. "I've learned just how powerless people are before a hurricane. From now on, if the experts say to leave, we'll go."

Nancy Pryor Williams and Sarah Williams - Pass Christian, Mississippi

For many people, a house seems like the safest place on earth. When it's raining or snowing, a house provides shelter. When it's cold, a house provides warmth. It's difficult to picture a house floating away like a sand castle from a beach. But that's just what happened to hundreds of houses during Hurricane Camille—including the one owned by Nancy Pryor Williams of Pass Christian, Mississippi.

Although her house stood only fifty feet from the Gulf of Mexico, Mrs. Williams ignored the warnings that were given all day Sunday. She felt that she and her three children—Sarah, Nancy Clay, and David—could survive the hurricane by taking refuge on the third floor. "I expected water on the first floor," Mrs. Williams explained long after her ordeal was over. "But I felt certain that the children and I would be safe upstairs."

As the hurricane neared the shore, the thirty-seven-year-old widow and her three children packed dishes and other valuables and moved them upstairs. They also took candles, water, food, and other emergency supplies upstairs.

"The water started coming in the house at about nine o'clock in the evening," remembered Sarah, who was twelve years old when Camille struck. "I was terrified when I saw it flooding the house." Soon much of the lower floor was under water. The family could see that it was just a matter of time before the water came up and drowned them or washed the house away.

At first, they were in a state of panic. They ran into David's room, prayed, and said good-bye to one another. Then, trembling in terror, Mrs. Williams realized she must act if her family were to have a chance.

She led the children to an upstairs bathroom. "I opened the window to look out, and the water was right at the level of the window—about twenty-two feet high. The bathroom was filling up higher and higher with water and the whole house was swaying from the water and the 190-mile-per-hour winds. I knew we had to get out of there. We had to go into that water."

Nancy Williams and the children were good swimmers. They took hold of the window frame and prepared to jump into the water. Then, suddenly, there was no need to jump. The entire house tilted. Then it tipped all the way over on its side and crashed into the water. Still holding onto the window frame and a chunk of the wall, the Williams family found themselves in the chilly water.

The four had a hard time holding onto the window frame. They were pelted by flying boards and tree limbs. Fourteen-year-old Nancy Clay was struck in the head by a board. "Ma, I can't hold on, I can't hold on!" she cried. Nancy Clay lost her

Nancy Pryor Williams

grip on the window frame. She fell into the water, but her mother and brother pulled her back up onto their little raft.

When the window frame was soaked with water, it started to sink. Mrs. Williams knew that they had to find something else to keep them afloat. "I was looking for a tree and I reached out to grab one. But the current was so strong that when I grabbed for the tree it nearly tore my arm off."

The family then spied a floating mattress. They held onto the mattress for a while, but it wasn't a very reliable raft. "Then this roof came bumping along and we climbed onto it," continued Sarah. "We lay on the rooftop for about six hours. We were freezing, so we lay next to each other for warmth. As we drifted hour after hour, we passed out from exhaustion."

At about five in the morning the rooftop lodged near the Bay St. Louis Bridge, about half a mile from where their home had stood. Summoning all their strength, the family climbed up onto the badly damaged bridge. Then they walked several miles to the town of Pass Christian.

*Left to right:
Nancy Clay, David,
and Sarah Williams*

They were barefooted, exhausted, and bleeding from their many cuts. A sharp object — later identified as a pine needle — had been driven deep into Mrs. Williams's chest by the wind. But none of the four was badly injured.

"When we went back to where our house had been, only the cement slab was left," said Sarah Williams. "But the only important thing was that we all survived. The material things could be replaced, but our lives couldn't."

George Michael Mixon - Pass Christian, Mississippi

When Hurricane Camille approached the Mississippi coast, the Mixon family split up into two parts. Mrs. Mixon and the two girls went to the hurricane shelter at the high school. Mr. Mixon and the two boys stayed at home.

George Michael Mixon, twenty-two years old at the time, was the oldest of the four children. That Sunday afternoon, he and his brother, Wayne, helped their father put furniture up on sawhorses in an effort to keep it dry. The Mixons had no idea that at about midnight their whole house would be washed away. "Close to ten o'clock, our front windows blew out," George Mixon remembered. "Water started coming into the house. We had to stand on the dining room table."

About an hour later, in came an even bigger wave. The Mixons knew that if they stayed in the house they might drown. Their father couldn't swim, so George and Wayne helped him get to the windowsill. The three then went out the window and climbed from the rising water up onto the roof. There they huddled together behind the chimney.

The roof gravel, hurled by the awful winds, pelted them like machine-gun fire. The heavy rain beat at them from every direction. The waves rolled up over their legs.

"I thought I'd die at any moment," George Michael Mixon continued. "I thought the house might break up and sink or that the next gust of wind would take us."

Things looked really bad for the Mixons. Then, at about midnight, their house broke away from its foundation and floated away. The walls and roof of the free-floating house were breaking up. The Mixons didn't know how long it would stay afloat. Fortunately, the house lodged against a big limb of a pine tree and stuck there.

The water went down at about five in the morning. Shortly after sunrise, the Mixons came down from their rooftop. They were very glad to be alive. But they still had a big worry. They didn't know what had become of Mrs. Mixon and the two girls who had taken refuge at the high school.

While walking to the high school with his father and brother, George Mixon looked around. "Our town looked like Berlin after it was bombed in World War II. Houses were reduced to piled-up boards. Highway 90 didn't even resemble

Left to right: George Michael Mixon, George M. Mixon, Jr., and Wayne S. Mixon

a road." The more they saw, the more worried they became.

At about seven in the morning, George, Wayne, and their dad completed the three-mile walk to the school. In a joyous meeting, they found that Mrs. Mixon and the two girls were safe. Only six inches of water had flowed into the school.

Today, George Michael Mixon is fire chief of Pass Christian. He is also the town's Civil Defense director. (The Civil Defense is an organization in the United States that works to save lives during times of disaster.) He visits area schools to tell children how to prepare for hurricanes.

"When the authorities tell you to evacuate—go!" Mixon advises. "Go and do not hesitate. You have to have the utmost respect for the wind and the water that come with hurricanes. Don't stay in a low-lying area as we did and think you can survive."

3/THE SCIENCE OF HURRICANES

Hurricanes Long Ago

Long ago, the people of Central America believed in a god named *Hurakán* who caused great storms. The storms were called *hurakáns*. When European explorers arrived in the Americas, they learned about these fierce storms. They changed the name to *hurricane*.

Christopher Columbus, credited with discovering America, had some bad experiences with hurricanes. In 1493, Columbus founded the first non-Indian town in the Americas. It was called Isabela, and it was built on the island of Hispaniola. Most people haven't heard of Isabela because it was soon wiped out by a hurricane.

Christopher Columbus encountered hurricanes during his voyages of discovery. On his third voyage, in 1498 (below), heavy seas threatened his ships.

In 1503, Columbus sailed into a hurricane off the coast of Central America. The following is Columbus's description of that storm:

> Eyes never beheld the seas so high, angry, and covered by foam. The wind not only prevented our progress, but offered no opportunity to run behind any headland for shelter. . . . Never did the sky look more terrible. . . . The lightning broke forth with such violence that each time I wondered if it had carried off my spars and sails; the flashes came with such fury and frightfulness that we all thought the ships would be blasted. All this time the water never ceased to fall from the sky. . . .

In past centuries, hurricanes sank many ships. In the late 1500s, Spain and England fought for control of the seas. The Spanish built a huge fleet of ships, called the Armada. The English defeated some of the Spanish ships, but others were wrecked by hurricanes.

The Spanish Armada (below) was defeated by both the English and the destructive force of hurricanes.

In 1620, the Pilgrims in the Mayflower *(above) encountered a storm, probably a hurricane, that diverted them to Massachusetts.*

Not only did Spain lose battleships to hurricanes, the country also lost many treasure ships. During the 1500s and 1600s, the treasure ships carried silver and gold from the Americas to Spain. More than a hundred of those ships were sunk by hurricanes. Many of them still lie on the ocean floor. From time to time, treasure hunters locate a sunken ship and bring its riches up to the surface.

England also had big problems with hurricanes. In 1607 the English built their first permanent settlement in America at Jamestown, Virginia. Two years later, a fleet of ships that set out for the new colony was caught in a hurricane. The survivors of the hurricane told stories that were heard around the world. These stories may have inspired famous playwright William Shakespeare to write *The Tempest*.

The Pilgrims sailed to America from England in 1620. They wanted to settle in Virginia. But they encountered a storm that was probably a hurricane. They went off course and wound up in Massachusetts.

English pirate William Dampier (right) discovered that hurricane winds move in a huge circle. He called a hurricane a "vast whirlwind."

Early Hurricane Science

Early explorers knew little about the storms that sank their ships and wrecked their newly built towns. One of the first discoveries regarding the nature of hurricanes was made in 1680 by English pirate William Dampier. Caught in a hurricane, Dampier's ship was blown for hundreds of miles. Yet when the storm had passed, Dampier found himself near the position where he had started. Dampier concluded that hurricane winds move in a huge circle. He said that a hurricane was a "vast whirlwind."

In 1821, an American named William Redfield found more proof of the circular wind action in hurricanes. While traveling through Massachusetts and Connecticut, Redfield saw trees that had been blown down by a hurricane. Some of the trees faced toward the northwest. Others pointed toward the southeast. From this Redfield deduced that hurricane winds must move in a circle.

As people began to understand more about hurricanes, they tried to give warnings of their approach. In 1865, a priest named Francisco Colina set up an observatory in the Philippines. From there, storm warnings were sent to Asia.

In 1870 another priest, Benito Viñes, built a hurricane observatory in Havana, Cuba. Father Benito, known as the "hurricane priest," asked sailors to notify him when they spotted a storm. Once he knew that a hurricane was coming, Father Benito sent warnings to the islands of the West Indies and the coast of the United States.

What Is a Hurricane?

Weather satellites have provided modern scientists with views of hurricanes from far out in space. Airplanes have allowed scientists to fly inside hurricanes. Using these and other tools, scientists now have an excellent idea of what a hurricane is.

A hurricane is a very big storm with winds that whip around in a giant circle. Hurricanes are similar to tornadoes, which also have rotating winds. Tornadoes, though, are much smaller—usually just several blocks wide or less. Hurricanes cover thousands of square miles.

On satellite pictures, a hurricane sometimes looks like a doughnut, a pinwheel, or a spiral galaxy. In the center of a hurricane is a calm part called the *eye*. The hurricane's winds rotate around the eye. The very strongest winds of the hurricane are located in the *wall clouds* that surround the eye. The winds in the wall clouds can reach 200 miles per hour or more. The wall clouds also produce the heaviest rain.

A hurricane has two kinds of motion. First there are the winds that swirl around at high speeds within the hurricane. Second, the entire storm moves forward at about 15 to 20 miles per hour.

Many of the hurricanes that strike our country begin as

In this satellite view (above) taken on September 12, 1979, Hurricane Frederic resembles a spiral galaxy. The horizontal radar view of Frederic (below) appeared on the screen of a research aircraft that same day.

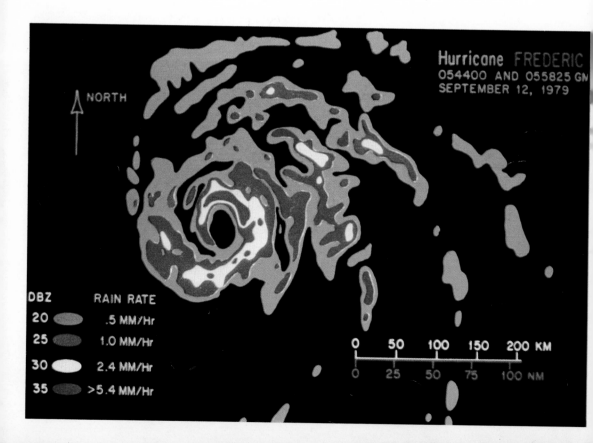

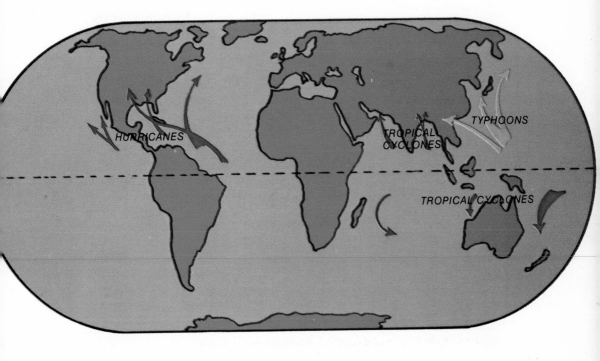

storms off the west coast of Africa. They churn slowly
westward until striking the West Indies and the southeastern
coast of the United States. Once over land, hurricanes usually
weaken and then disappear.

The United States isn't the only place that gets battered by
these fierce storms. But in other parts of the world they have
different names. In the North Pacific Ocean they are called
typhoons. In the Indian Ocean and the South Pacific Ocean
they are called *tropical cyclones*. Hurricanes, typhoons, and
tropical cyclones are all the same kind of storm with different
names.

How Hurricanes Are Formed

It is not known for sure how hurricanes are formed. But the ingredients that go into making a hurricane are known. Some of the main ingredients are:

- ocean water
- the heat of the sun
- air
- wind
- the spin of the earth

Scientists have various theories (ideas) to explain how these ingredients make a hurricane. According to the theory accepted by most scientists, it all starts when the heat of the sun warms some ocean water. The evaporating water forms a cloud of warm, wet air that moves upward.

As this warm, moist air rises, more air rushes in to replace it. This air is also heated and moistened by the warm ocean surface. It begins to rise and form clouds, heating the air around it. Eventually, a large mass of warm, moist air with rain clouds is formed over the ocean. Because the air is warm, it expands. It becomes less dense and lighter, and forms an area of low pressure. More air near the ocean surface now rushes in. However, this air doesn't just flow straight in like water flowing downhill. It spirals in like water going down a bathtub drain. This spiral, or spinning motion, is caused by the rotation of the earth. The air goes faster and faster as it spirals inward. Then it rises in the clouds to form an eye and wall clouds. The whole storm, now spinning like a top, is carried across the ocean by the wind. Finally, it moves over land or cold water. It loses it fuel source (warm ocean) or encounters other unfavorable surroundings, and dies, often leaving a path of destruction in its wake.

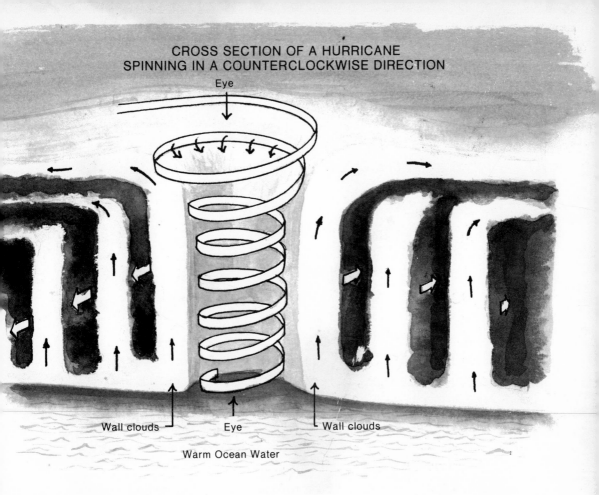

CROSS SECTION OF A HURRICANE
SPINNING IN A COUNTERCLOCKWISE DIRECTION

Eye

Wall clouds   Eye   Wall clouds

Warm Ocean Water

How Hurricanes Kill and Destroy

The power of a hurricane is almost beyond imagination. If
the energy of a single hurricane could be changed into
electricity, the United States would have all the power it
needed for three years. Unfortunately, we don't have the
ability to transform a hurricane's power into electricity.
Instead, the power sometimes kills human beings and wrecks
cities.

Many people think of wind when they think of hurricanes.
The great winds in hurricanes send tree limbs and other
objects flying through the air. These flying objects account for
some of the deaths in hurricanes. But wind-blown debris
causes a very low percentage of hurricane deaths.

Water is by far the biggest killer in a hurricane. You will remember that the wind piles up huge amounts of water along the shorelines. The water rolls across the coast and drowns people. The rising water is called a *storm surge*. Storm surges account for 90 percent of the deaths in hurricanes.

Even after a hurricane moves inland and starts to die, its clouds can release tremendous amounts of rain. Sometimes these rains end droughts and are welcome. At other times the rains create deadly floods. You will remember that floods caused by Camille killed more than 100 people in Virginia and West Virginia.

Hurricanes have one more way to kill and destroy. Tornadoes often dip down from a hurricane's storm clouds. Hurricane Beulah, in 1967, produced 115 separate tornadoes in Texas. During Hurricane Camille, in 1969, one tornado lifted a house above 75-foot trees and set it down 2½ miles from its foundation.

In the next chapter you will see these killers at work in some very well-known hurricanes.

The rising water from a storm surge at Biscayne Bay lashes the Miami shore during a 1948 hurricane.

Two-foot normal high tide

Normal sea level

HIGH TIDE TWENTY-FOUR HOURS BEFORE STORM SURGE

Five-foot high tide

Normal sea level

HIGH TIDE TWELVE HOURS BEFORE STORM SURGE

THE FORMATION AND EFFECTS OF A HURRICANE STORM SURGE

Twenty-four hours before a storm surge reaches the Gulf Coast, tides are normal. A hurricane has developed, however, and this area is under a Hurricane Watch.

Twelve hours before the hurricane hits, the tide is three or four feet above normal and the wind speed is increasing.

When the hurricane reaches the coast (below), there is a fifteen-foot surge added to the normal two-foot high tide, creating a seventeen-foot storm tide. This great mound of water, topped by battering waves, is the hurricane's most deadly killer.

Seventeen-foot storm tide
(normal high tide plus storm surge)

Fifteen-foot storm surge

Two-foot normal high tide

Normal sea level

HIGH TIDE AT PEAK OF STORM SURGE

4/SOME MAJOR HURRICANES

Galveston, Texas - 1900

In the early 1800s, pirate Jean Laffite made his headquarters on Galveston Island, in the Gulf of Mexico. The island—a flat sandbar—was a perfect pirate's den. From his fort, Laffite could see ships passing in all directions. When he spied a ship, Laffite and his men sailed off to rob it.

A few years after the United States Navy drove Laffite away, other people saw that Galveston Island was a fine place to live. In 1839, a city was built on the island. This city was named Galveston.

Galveston grew. By 1900, 38,000 people lived there. Cotton products and flour were made in the city. Many products came into the United States through Galveston's port.

Besides being an important manufacturing and port city, Galveston was also a popular vacation spot. Each year, thousands came to enjoy its sandy beaches. The "Queen City," as it was called, had fancy hotels, fine restaurants, huge mansions, and tree-lined streets.

In the years before 1900, Galveston often had been struck by hurricanes. One in 1837 had delayed the founding of the town. An 1842 hurricane had knocked over half the town's buildings. But in 1900 most people thought that Galveston's houses and big buildings could withstand any hurricane.

In early September of 1900, a hurricane moved in from the Atlantic Ocean and struck Cuba. By September 6 the storm was lashing Florida's coast. Then suddenly it changed direction. It headed west—directly for Galveston.

Isaac M. Cline, chief of Galveston's Weather Bureau, was warned of the approaching storm. Dr. Cline took out the storm-warning flag—red with a black center—and raised it above the Weather Bureau building.

Early on the morning of September 8, the outskirts of the hurricane moved into Galveston. Gray, heavy clouds filled the sky. Rain fell. Dr. Cline knew that the winds of the hurricane were likely to push huge waves into Galveston. He got into a horse-drawn wagon and went along Galveston's beaches. "Move to higher ground!" he told people. Cline knew that the highest ground on the whole island was only nine feet above sea level. But that was better than the beach.

Few people left their homes for higher ground. Even those who expected a flood thought their homes could survive it.

The wind speed rose from 30 to 70 miles per hour on that terrible Saturday. When the gusts reached 120 miles per hour, the wind gauge was blown off the Weather Bureau building. Trees snapped. Telephone and telegraph lines went down. Roof tiles flew through the air like deadly hatchets. Soon the bridges leading out of Galveston were wrecked. The city was completely cut off from the rest of the world.

The fury of the 1900 hurricane flung ships from the Galveston harbor.

Then came the worst part. As people looked out their windows, they saw rising water moving over the beaches and on into the city. The water rushed into living rooms and sent people running up stairs. Even up high the screaming and crying people weren't safe. Smashed repeatedly by the waves, houses broke loose from the ground and swirled away.

Many people inside the houses were drowned. Some jumped out windows and swam for their lives. They grasped for trees, rooftops, and other floating debris.

Weatherman Isaac Cline watched the water rise higher and higher against his own house. Cline had built the house to resist hurricanes. Knowing this, about fifty neighbors had come there for shelter. Houses near Cline's were smashed by the waves. The wreckage crashed against the Cline house. Finally, it, too, collapsed into the water.

Cline's pregnant wife and about thirty other people were drowned. But Dr. Cline and his daughter escaped the house through a hole in the roof. Two other Cline children jumped out a window and took refuge with their father on the floating roof.

Above: An aerial view of Galveston Island today.
Below: A train nearly topples from the force of the water during the 1900 hurricane.

Above: The Bath Avenue Free School and Old Woman's Home after the Galveston hurricane.

Below: The Galveston Island seawall was built to protect the city from flooding during future hurricanes.

There were many other amazing survival stories. One girl, Anna Delz, was flung into the water when her house collapsed. Anna grabbed a tree and floated with it for a while. Then she grabbed onto a roof that came floating along. When the roof began to crumble, she held onto a big piece of wood. Mile after mile she floated. Anna Delz was carried to safety eighteen miles from Galveston.

The waves were so powerful that ships were flung from Galveston's harbor. One, the *Taunton,* was thrown onto the Texas mainland in Chambers County, twenty-two miles from Galveston.

Late on the evening of September 8, the hurricane moved out of Galveston. As the water went down, the stunned survivors saw thousands of bodies in the muck. A total of at least 7,200 people lay dead in and around Galveston. That is the highest death toll the United States has ever had in a natural disaster.

Galveston was rebuilt. But its people knew that future hurricanes could wreck their city again. The people decided to do something to prevent that. A huge seawall was built to protect Galveston. The wall was built to a greater height than the tallest waves of the 1900 hurricane.

In 1915 another hurricane struck Galveston. The winds were so strong that a ship was picked up and tossed over the seawall. Water overflowed the wall and poured into the city. But the seawall protected Galveston from the terrible flooding that had occurred in 1900. Although 275 persons died in Texas and Louisiana, only eight lives were lost in Galveston. The seawall built to protect Galveston is still there today. However, some hard lessons learned long ago seem to have been forgotten. Buildings are now going up on the sea side of the seawall.

Florida's Lake Okeechobee - 1928

In early September of 1928, people in Florida listened to radio reports about a hurricane that was battering Puerto Rico. United States weather experts advised people on the east coast of Florida to seek shelter. Just two years earlier, a terrible hurricane had killed several hundred persons in Miami. Remembering that, people boarded up their windows and sought shelter in strong buildings.

On Sunday, September 16, the sky turned gray and rain fell in southeastern Florida. The storm tore off roofs and knocked down trees in the coastal city of West Palm Beach. Usually, hurricanes do their greatest harm along the coast. But this hurricane surprised everyone by heading inland, toward Lake Okeechobee in southern Florida. Okeechobee is a very shallow lake, with an average depth of seven feet. But it is a huge one—about 700 square miles. In 1928, about 6,000 persons lived around the lake in small communities.

When the winds came, people headed into their flimsy houses and boarded them up. After the wind destroyed their homes, people grabbed hold of chimneys and trees to keep from being blown away.

As the wind blasted at the shallow lake, the water at one end was pushed toward the other side. The water overflowed the lake and flooded the towns. Houses that had withstood the wind floated away.

Those people who hadn't drowned climbed high into trees to escape the floods. But they weren't the only ones seeking shelter. Thousands of water moccasins had curled themselves around the trees. The snakes were fleeing the rising waters, too. Some people who had survived the wind and the flood died of snakebite.

The hurricane that struck Lake Okeechobee killed approximately 2,000 people. (No one is sure of the exact figure.) On just one portion of road near the lake, 200 bodies were found. Decades later, farmers were still finding skeletons of the storm's victims.

New England - 1938

In the early 1900s, the great storms were known as "Florida hurricanes." That was because most of the big ones of recent years had hit the state of Florida. Many people thought it was almost impossible for a hurricane to strike the Atlantic coast as far north as New England. When a hurricane smashed Rhode Island and other New England states in 1938, almost everyone was taken by surprise.

The hurricane was first noticed on September 16, 1938, when a ship encountered it in the Atlantic Ocean. The storm headed up toward Florida but missed its eastern coast. It was expected that the hurricane would swing eastward and then fizzle out over the cold waters of the North Atlantic Ocean. In 1938 there were no satellites to monitor the movement of the hurricane. After missing Florida, the hurricane headed northward. It struck the northeastern United States on September 21.

First the hurricane smashed into the coast of New Jersey. Wind and waves damaged houses, knocked down trees and telephone poles, and wrecked crops. A bridge connecting Atlantic City to an offshore island was destroyed. All this was relatively light damage for a hurricane. But as the storm continued northward, it became a killer.

On the beaches of Long Island, New York, some hardy

The 1938 New England hurricane ruined these homes in Westhampton, Long Island.

people were trying to swim in the tall waves. Suddenly a 20-foot storm wave struck the island and swept the beaches clear. The waves hit Long Island with such force that the island actually shook. The shocks were detected on earthquake instruments 3,000 miles away.

Long Island protects southwestern Connecticut like a giant seawall. But the shore of southeastern Connecticut was pounded by the hurricane.

At the seaside town of Stonington, Connecticut, it appeared that some tracks would give way and tumble a train into the rising flood. The passengers piled into the front car and the rest of the train was cut loose. The single car made it safely over the weak tracks to dry land.

Hurricane damage in the business section of Providence, Rhode Island.

Rhode Island, the smallest state in the country, was hit hardest by the hurricane. As hundreds of seaside houses swirled into the water, many people drowned. In Jamestown, Rhode Island, a school bus had to stop on a road because of the high water. The children formed a line, held hands, and tried to cross the road. Suddenly a storm wave came up and washed the children and the driver into the water. Seven of the children drowned.

Providence—the largest city in Rhode Island—was hit very hard. Located at the top of Narragansett Bay, the city was flooded when the winds drove the water up the bay. As water rushed into downtown buildings, people ran to higher floors. Watching from high above the city, they could see car headlights shining under the water. Later it was learned that twelve feet of water had covered downtown Providence.

The highest wind speed measured in this hurricane occurred at Blue Hills Observatory in Massachusetts. There the winds reached 183 miles per hour—one of the highest recorded wind speeds of any hurricane ever. At Boston, there were wind gusts of 100 miles per hour. The wind and waves killed dozens of people in Massachusetts.

By the time the New England Hurricane fizzled out over Canada on the following morning, approximately 600 people were dead. About 1,800 had been injured.

The people of New England—and United States weather experts—learned a lesson from this terrible hurricane. They now knew that hurricanes could strike New England with as much force as they strike Florida. After this, buildings put up near the ocean were built with extra care. Seawalls were built to protect cities from floods. New England has been hit by other hurricanes since 1938. None, as yet, has been as deadly as the New England Hurricane of 1938. Many more people now live along the coast, however. Today, a major hurricane like the 1938 storm would be devastating to New England.

The 1938 New England hurricane tossed this two-masted schooner onto a pier in Fairhaven, Massachusetts.

East Pakistan - 1970

The storms that we call hurricanes are called cyclones in the Bay of Bengal. When the people of East Pakistan (now Bangladesh) heard talk that a cyclone was about to strike in November of 1970, they weren't surprised. Only the month before, a cyclone had killed several hundred people. In the past ten years, eight cyclones had struck. The people, mostly poor farmers, were given very little warning about this monstrous new cyclone. A warning wouldn't have helped them much, however. They had no transportation and no place to go.

The cyclone whirled into East Pakistan on the rainy night of November 12, 1970. People sleeping in their huts were awakened by a tremendous roar. Winds of 120 miles per hour were driving the waters of the Bay of Bengal toward the islands and coastal towns. When people rushed outside to see what was happening they could hardly believe their eyes. They saw what appeared to be a wall of water 25 feet high.

Thousands upon thousands of people were swept away and drowned. Some lucky ones grabbed for trees and hung on tightly. On one island, Munshi Mustansher Billa and his family grabbed hold of palm trees outside their hut. One by one, Munshi's five children lost their grip on the trees and drowned. Finally, only Munshi, his wife, and the baby Munshi was holding were left alive. As the hours passed and the wind and water battered at them, Munshi's hands turned numb. He lost his grip and his infant son slipped into the water. "I couldn't hold on to him!" he cried to his wife. Only Munshi and his wife survived.

Some people survived the water by holding onto the tails of cattle or floating on bamboo poles. In one town a man stuffed his six grandchildren into a wooden chest, then climbed in himself. When they reached shore three days later the grandfather was dead, but the six children were safe.

As the waters receded, thousands of dead bodies were seen lying in the mud. In some communities, not one person or animal was left alive. "No vulture, no dog, and even no insects were to be found anywhere—just heaps of human bodies," one Pakistani official said after looking at the coastline.

No one knows exactly how many died in this cyclone, but the number almost certainly topped 500,000. Of all the hurricanes, typhoons, and cyclones to strike our planet in recorded history, this was the deadliest. Except for an earthquake that shook China in 1976, it was this century's deadliest natural disaster of any kind.

SOME MAJOR TYPHOON, CYCLONE, AND HURRICANE DISASTERS OUTSIDE THE UNITED STATES

Type of Storm	Date	Places Hardest Hit	Approximate Number of Deaths
Hurricane	November 26-27, 1703	England	8,000
Cyclone	October 5, 1864	Calcutta, India	70,000
Cyclone	October 31, 1876	Bakarganj, India	200,000
Typhoon	October 8, 1881	Indochina	300,000
Cyclone	June 5, 1882	Bombay, India	100,000
Hurricane	August 8, 1899	Puerto Rico	3,400
Typhoon	September 18, 1906	Hong Kong	10,000
Hurricane	September 3, 1930	Santo Domingo, Dominican Republic	2,000
Typhoon	September 21, 1934	Honshu, Japan	4,000
Cyclone	October 16, 1942	Bengal, India	40,000
Two cyclones	October 10 and October 31, 1960	East Pakistan (now Bangladesh)	14,000
Cyclone	May 28-29, 1963	East Pakistan (now Bangladesh)	22,000
Hurricane Flora	October 1-9, 1963	Haiti and Cuba	7,000
Cyclone	May 12, 1965	East Pakistan (now Bangladesh)	13,000
Cyclone	December 15, 1965	East Pakistan (now Bangladesh)	25,000
Cyclone	November 12-13, 1970	East Pakistan (now Bangladesh)	At least 500,000 (the most ever killed by any kind of storm)
Hurricane Fifi	September 19-20, 1974	Honduras	8,000
Cyclone	November 19, 1977	India	15,000

Near Choloma, Honduras, a young man carrying his bicycle trudges through water left by Hurricane Fifi in September, 1974.

SOME MAJOR UNITED STATES HURRICANES

Date	Places Hardest Hit	Deaths	Comments
August 27-28, 1893	South Carolina	More than 1,000	
October 1-2, 1893	Louisiana, Mississippi, and Alabama	More than 1,000	
August 27-September 15, 1900	Galveston, Texas	At least 7,200	The worst natural disaster in U.S. history
September 10-21, 1909	Louisiana and Mississippi	350	
August 5-25, 1915	Texas and Louisiana	275	
September 22-October 1, 1915	Gulf Coast	275	
September 2-15, 1919	Florida, Louisiana, and Texas	287	About 500 more lives were lost in ships at sea
September 11-22, 1926	Florida and Alabama	243	Most of the deaths were in the Miami area
September 6-20, 1928	Southern Florida	Approximately 2,000	Almost all of the deaths occurred at Lake Okeechobee
August 29-September 10, 1935 (called the Labor Day Hurricane)	Southern Florida	408	This storm produced winds of 200 miles per hour; during the storm the barometer fell to 26.35 inches, the lowest reading ever in the Western Hemisphere
September 10-22, 1938 (the New England Hurricane)	Long Island and southern New England	Approximately 600	Moving forward at speeds of over 50 miles per hour, this hurricane was extremely destructive
August 7-21, 1955 (Hurricane Diane)	North Carolina up to New England	184	Rainfall caused bad flooding in New England
June 25-28, 1957 (Hurricane Audrey)	Louisiana, Mississippi, and Texas	390	This storm killed 371 in Louisiana alone
August 14-22, 1969 (Hurricane Camille)	Mississippi, Louisiana, Alabama, Virginia, and West Virginia	324	Winds topped 200 miles per hour
June 14-23, 1972 (Hurricane Agnes)	From Florida all the way up to New York	122	This storm produced tornadoes and bad floods
August 29-September 14, 1979 (Hurricane Frederic)	Alabama and Mississippi	15	Excellent warning system and public response accounted for low death toll in what was an extremely destructive hurricane

50

Henderson House, one of the most beautiful homes on the Gulf Coast, was destroyed by Hurricane Camille.

5/PROTECTING OURSELVES FROM HURRICANES

Since the year 1900, more than 13,000 Americans have died in hurricanes. Eleven thousand of those people died between 1900 and 1939. Fewer than 2,000 of them died between 1940 and 1980. The number of deaths has dropped in recent decades because the United States has improved its hurricane warning methods.

Meteorologists (weather scientists) at the National Hurricane Center in Miami, Florida have helped keep the yearly toll low. "Our job is to provide hurricane forecasts and warnings for the United States, Central America, and the Caribbean Sea," explains Dr. Robert Sheets, who is a hurricane forecaster at the Center. "Our number-one goal is to prevent loss of life."

The scientists at the National Hurricane Center have a number of tools that help them make their predictions:

- Weather satellites, 22,000 miles out in space, send pictures of our planet's cloud patterns to the National Hurricane Center. Hurricane clouds can be seen plainly on these pictures. The satellite pictures tell the scientists which direction the storm is traveling. They also show the size of the hurricane.

- In 1943, Colonel Joseph P. Duckworth became the first person to make a planned airplane flight into a hurricane. Duckworth's plane was bounced around quite a bit, but it survived the flight. Today scientists at the National Hurricane Center regularly send airplanes into the great storms. The pilots, some of whom are called

"Hurricane Hunters," have been specially trained to fly the propeller-driven airplanes.

Instruments aboard the aircraft measure the wind speeds, wind direction, air pressure, rainfall rates, and temperature of the hurricane. The flights are often bumpy. It is difficult for the meteorologists aboard the planes to make the readings themselves. So computers send the information to the National Hurricane Center. There scientists carefully study the data to get an even better idea of the power and movement of the storm.

- The coasts of the United States are blanketed by a network of radar. The radar signals bounce off raindrops in the sky, thereby showing places where there are hurricanes and other storms. New systems allow many of the coastal radar station signals to be transmitted and displayed at the National Hurricane Center as they occur.

- Weather balloons, ships at sea, and observers along the coasts also provide information for the scientists at the National Hurricane Center.

The forecasters at the Center carefully study all this information. When they think that a hurricane will strike the United States coast within two days, they issue what is called a *hurricane watch*. A hurricane watch means that there is a threat of a hurricane and that people should watch and listen carefully for instructions. Hurricanes don't always move in an easily predictable way. They change directions, curve, and sometimes even stand still. For that reason, the hurricane watch is given for a larger area than may actually be struck by

*This National Oceanic and Atmospheric Administration
research aircraft is used for penetration of hurricanes.*

the storm. Hurricane watch information—and other news of
the storm—is broadcast on radio and television and printed in
newspapers.

As the hurricane moves closer to land, the forecasters are
better able to tell which cities are in danger. When the storm
is about twelve daylight hours from striking land, a *hurricane
warning* is given. A hurricane warning is extremely serious.
When one is issued for a specific area, there is an excellent
chance that it will be hit. When local officials receive the
hurricane warning information, they may advise people to
leave the area.

What To Do When a Hurricane Approaches

People who live in inland cities such as Chicago, Cleveland, Omaha, or Denver need not worry about hurricanes. But anyone who lives along the Atlantic Ocean or the Gulf of Mexico should know what to do in case of a hurricane.

June 1 through the end of November is the main hurricane season in the United States. Before June 1, people in hurricane-prone areas should find out how high their houses stand above sea level. They should know all the roads that lead inland in case they have to leave in a hurry. They should make sure they have a battery-powered radio so that they can hear weather reports even if the electricity is knocked out. In addition, they should store fresh drinking water in jugs and stock up on canned foods in case they must spend several days at home without electrical power. From June 1 through November they should watch the news to see if there are any signs of hurricanes.

Meteorologist and hurricane forecaster Dr. Robert C. Sheets on the job at the National Hurricane Center forecast center.

If a hurricane watch is given for a city or town, then the people who live there should be alert to the danger. The National Weather Service advises people to do the following in the event of a *hurricane watch:*

- Keep listening to the television or radio for further bulletins.
- Get the car ready to go; people who don't have a car should make sure that they can leave by some other form of transportation.
- Make preparations for fresh drinking water and other emergency supplies.
- Gather materials for boarding or taping up windows to prevent them from breaking.
- Make preparations for securing outdoor belongings such as boats and lawn furniture.

Saving human lives is the main goal in the event of a hurricane. So it is extremely important to listen closely to the weather bulletins. If the hurricane watch is changed to a hurricane warning, you know that things are really getting serious. The National Weather Service gives the following advice for times of *hurricane warnings:*

- The moment local officials advise you to leave your home, GO! Head inland (away from the water) or go to a storm shelter in your town. In general, people who live very close to the shoreline or on offshore islands should leave. People who live near a river or in an area that floods should leave. People who live near the coast in mobile homes should leave because mobile homes are very vulnerable to flooding and high winds.
- If you stay in your house during a hurricane, don't get fooled when the eye passes over. Remember, this is the calm part of the storm. After the eye passes over there will be more terrible winds.
- Make sure that people and pets are inside.
- Listen continually for weather bulletins.
- Secure boats and lawn furniture.
- Move valuable items to the upper floors of your house.

- Tape or board windows and doors; wedge sliding glass doors with a bar. Draw all drapes and blinds.
- As the hurricane approaches, stay away from windows.

A Success Story - Hurricane Frederic

In late August of 1979, satellite pictures showed a storm forming over the Atlantic Ocean. On September 1, its winds topped 74 miles per hour. It was named Hurricane Frederic.

When Hurricane Frederic approached the coast, the National Hurricane Center sent up airplanes to study it. It was learned that Frederic had winds of 140 miles per hour. Clearly it was a very dangerous storm.

Scientists at the National Hurricane Center studied the satellite pictures, the information gathered by airplanes, and other data. At 6:00 P.M. on Tuesday, September 11, they issued a hurricane watch for an area extending from Florida

This Hurricane Frederic satellite picture taken by GOES (Geostationary Operational Environmental Satellite) helped scientists forecast the hurricane and warn residents who might be in the path of the storm.

Left, top and bottom: A Gulf Shores, Alabama condominium before and after Hurricane Frederic. Below: A home in Mobile, Alabama after Hurricane Frederic.

to Louisiana. At 9:30, the watch was changed to a hurricane warning. The area warned extended from Panama City, Florida to Grand Isle, Louisiana. People listening to their radios or television sets heard the following message:

RESIDENTS OF LOW COASTAL AREAS AND OFFSHORE ISLANDS SHOULD BE PREPARED TO RESPOND QUICKLY IN CASE EVACUATION ORDERS ARE ISSUED BY LOCAL OFFICIALS WEDNESDAY MORNING.

Most people in the southeastern United States listened closely for further bulletins. On the morning of Wednesday, September 12, local officials advised people in low-lying coastal areas and offshore islands to evacuate. They were told: LEAVE BEFORE ESCAPE ROUTES BECOME FLOODED. It was expected that Frederic would hit land sometime that evening.

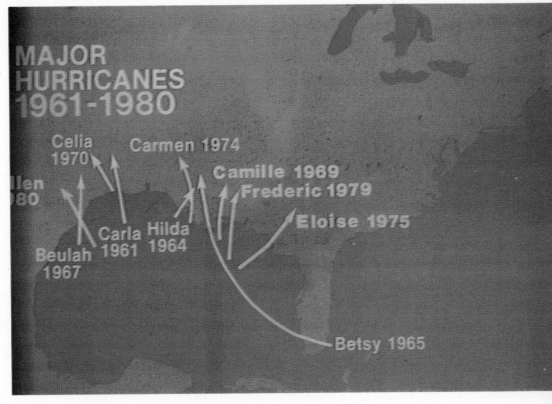

MAJOR
HURRICANES
1961-1980

Celia 1970

Carmen 1974

Camille 1969

Frederic 1979

Eloise 1975

Carla 1961

Hilda 1964

Beulah 1967

llen 80

Betsy 1965

Tracks of the major hurricanes to strike the United States between 1961 and 1980.

Before nightfall, 250,000 persons left the coast and moved inland. Frederic struck at about 10:00 P.M. The coasts of Alabama and Mississippi were slammed the hardest. A storm surge of about 10 feet flooded the coast. At Dauphin Island in Alabama, winds of 145 miles per hour were reported. A dozen tornadoes also were spawned by Frederic. The storm surge, wind, and tornadoes caused 2.3 billion dollars worth of damage. That made it the costliest hurricane in United States history—in terms of money.

"A thousand lives could have been lost in Hurricane Frederic if there had been no warnings," says Dr. Robert Sheets of the National Hurricane Center. But because there were warnings and because people listened to them, only fifteen persons were killed by this mighty hurricane.

Future Hurricanes

Despite the fact that the death toll from hurricanes has gone way down in recent years, hurricane experts are worried about the future. First, there is concern over the ever-increasing population in coastal areas. In 1900, fewer than 20 million people lived near the coastlines of the Atlantic Ocean and the Gulf of Mexico. Today, the population of those coastal regions is more than 60 million. As the number of people increases, hurricanes have a bigger human target.

Hurricane experts fear that some of those people will not leave their homes when they are so advised. "People who have lived along the coast for a long time and have seen bad hurricanes tend to take action," says Dr. Robert Sheets. "Those who have just moved to the coast tend to be terrified of hurricanes, and they also leave when a warning is given. The problem is with people who have been there ten years or so and have perhaps experienced just a fringe of a hurricane. They may think it won't be so bad and decide to stay home when a bad one hits."

Another problem is that buildings have gone up in potentially dangerous places. Housing developments now stand on islands that have previously been wiped clean by hurricanes. In some cases, only one bridge leads to the mainland. Should the bridge be knocked out at the start of the hurricane, the people would be left with no way to escape.

"The chances of a given area being struck by a hurricane are small, and we are not saying that people should avoid living in coastal areas," says Dr. Sheets. "We do think that people should know the dangers of hurricanes.

"We at the National Hurricane Center are working to educate people about those dangers. The general public,

Top left: Hurricane
Audry piled up a
fishing boat named
Audry *near a ruined home
in Cameron, Louisiana.*

*Above: Hurricane
Beulah made a shambles
of this grocery store
in Fulton, Texas.*

*Increasing populations
in coastal areas give
hurricanes bigger
human targets.
Seashore villages such
as the one pictured
(left) have no protection
against the force of
the wind-whipped waves.*

government officials, builders, local planners, and
community leaders should know about the dangers. For
example, communities should make sure that there are
adequate highways to evacuate the area if necessary.
Buildings should be constructed with hurricane safety in
mind.

"It may be impossible to eliminate loss of life totally during
hurricanes. But if people plan for them and follow directions
when a warning is given, very few need die."

Glossary

Cyclone, tropical The name for a hurricane that occurs in the Indian Ocean or the South Pacific Ocean

Disaster A sudden, destructive event that causes great damage and loss

Evacuate To leave a threatened area for protection

Evaporate To change from water to vapor

Eye, hurricane The calm center of a hurricane

Flood A body of water that overflows and covers land that is normally dry

Hurricane A huge, powerful windstorm that whirls in a circular motion and covers thousands of square miles; it is much larger than a tornado, but its winds are not as strong

Forecast , weather The prediction of what future weather conditions will be

Hurricane hunter A pilot of a research airplane used for studying hurricanes

Hurricane warning A message from a local weather office stating that a hurricane is expected to strike a specific place within the next twelve hours

Hurricane watch A message from a local weather office stating that a hurricane is expected to strike an area within two days

Meteorologist A weather scientist

Observatory, weather A place from which scientists study weather conditions

Radar An instrument that can detect and locate distant objects by means of reflected radio waves

Rotate Spin

Seawall A wall or embankment built at a shoreline to protect an area from flooding

Spiral motion The spinning motion of a hurricane

Storm surge A great mound of water, topped by battering waves, that moves toward shore during a hurricane

Storm warning flag A square red flag with a solid black square in the center. When one flag is hoisted, there is a storm warning for the area; when two flags are hoisted, one above the other, there is a hurricane warning for the area.

Tide The regular rise and fall of ocean waters caused by the gravitation, or pull, of the moon and the sun

Tornado A violently whirling column of air that descends from a thundercloud system and touches the ground; it is the most powerful and destructive storm on earth

Typhoon The name for a hurricane that occurs in the North Pacific Ocean

Wall clouds or eyewall clouds The storm clouds that surround the eye of a hurricane and produce the strongest winds and heaviest rain of the hurricane

Weather balloon A balloon that carries instruments aloft to measure the temperature, moisture, and pressure characteristics in the upper air

Weather satellite An instrument that orbits thousands of miles above the earth and takes pictures of cloud formations which are relayed to weather stations on the ground

Index
Page numbers that appear in boldface type indicate illustrations.

Photo Credits

About the Author

Dennis Fradin attended Northwestern University on a partial creative writing
scholarship and graduated in 1967. He has published stories and articles in such places
as *Ingenue, The Saturday Evening Post, Scholastic, Chicago, Oui,* and *National Humane
Review.* His previous books include the Young People's Stories of Our States series
for Childrens Press and *Bad Luck Tony* for Prentice-Hall. He is married and the
father of three children.

About the Artist

Len Meents studied painting and drawing at Southern Illinois University and after
graduation in 1969 he moved to Chicago. Mr. Meents works full time as a painter and
illustrator. He and his wife and their two children currently make their home in
LaGrange, Illinois.

551.5
F

Fradin, Dennis B.

Hurricanes

DATE DUE

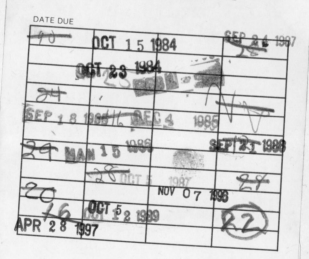

90	OCT 1 5 1984	SEP 2 4 1997
	OCT 23 1984	
24		
SEP 1 8 1985	DEC 4 1985	NV
24 MAR 1 5 1986		SEP 2 1 1988
20	28 OCT 5 1987 NOV 0 7 1996	24
16 OCT 5 2 1989 APR 2 8 1997		22